MUSIC CITY RHYTHM & BLUES
REVISITED

COUNTRY MUSIC FOUNDATION PRESS

222 REP. JOHN LEWIS WAY S · NASHVILLE, TENNESSEE 37203

First edition 2004. Revised edition 2024. Printed in the United States of America.

978-0-915608-44-7

This publication was created by the staff of the Country Music Hall of Fame® and Museum.

Original Exhibition Curators: Daniel Cooper and Michael Gray · Editors: Paul Kingsbury and Michael Gray

Printer: Lithographics, Inc., Nashville, Tennessee

CONTENTS

OPPOSITE PAGE: Detail from the Gibson ES-345 of Johnny Jones.
COURTESY OF JIMMY CHURCH. ARTIFACT PHOTO BY BOB DELEVANTE

COVER PHOTO: Frank Howard & the Commanders with guitarist Johnny Jones. (l to r)
Charlie Fite, Herschel Carter, Frank Howard, and Johnny Jones, mid-1960s.
COURTESY OF FRANK HOWARD

BACK COVER PHOTO: Nashville singer Willie Lee Patton, 1940s.
COURTESY OF IRENE (JACKSON) IRVIN

INSIDE COVER IMAGES: Screenshots from the stage set of *The!!!!Beat*, 1966.

DEAR MUSEUM FRIEND,

ABOVE AND OPPOSITE PAGE: **Stage wear designed and made by Richard Johnson for singer and bandleader Jimmy Church.**

COURTESY OF JIMMY CHURCH
ARTIFACT PHOTO BY BOB DELEVANTE

Twenty years ago, the Museum opened a groundbreaking exhibition, *Night Train to Nashville: Music City Rhythm & Blues, 1945–1970*, and released a two-disc set by that name. In both the exhibition and the CD/LP set, the Museum conducted extensive research to examine a time when the capital of country music was also a mecca for R&B musicians and their fans. The exhibition was subsequently honored by the NAACP with the "Bridging the Gap" award for promoting interracial understanding, and the album won a Grammy.

While Nashville's contributions to country music have been documented extensively, the city's far-reaching rhythm & blues legacy is still not as well known. Through the *Night Train to Nashville* exhibition, recordings, and publications such as this one, and through accompanying Museum programs, we hope you will have ample opportunity to engage with this rarely told part of Nashville's music history.

As is the case throughout our museum, we have made every effort to let the music of *Night Train to Nashville* tell its own story. Just as the sound of vintage Nashville R&B informs the exhibition, so too we hope your experience of the music, and the history it represents, will remain with you. We are proud to revisit this exhibition, and we are grateful to the men and women whose talent, struggle, and conviction gave us a story so important and exciting to tell. So, enjoy *Night Train to Nashville*. Thank you for getting on board.

Sincerely,

Kyle Young | CEO

ACKNOWLEDGMENTS

We hope this companion book and the exhibition it accompanies, *Night Train to Nashville: Music City Rhythm & Blues Revisited*, conveys the importance of the music made in the city and its story to the world. In fact, the world of popular music would sound quite different without this crucial chapter.

Nashville led the way in the broadcast of groundbreaking R&B on radio station WLAC and on TV shows *Night Train* and *The!!!!Beat*, casting the music across the country, influencing countless performers and songwriters, and the greater public.

The book and exhibition reflect collaboration between many friends and associates of the Country Music Hall of Fame and Museum. We are grateful to them all, and to those who have loaned artifacts, documents, instruments, stagewear and photographs, which have brought the exhibition and book to life.

We wish to thank Levert Allison, the family of Noble Blackwell, Misti Bragg, William Burney, John Carr, Alison Davis, Andrenee Majors Douglas, David Ewing, Peggy Gaines, Mark Hawkins, Dan Heller, the McCrary Sisters, Dr. Bryan Pierce, Sandra "King" Stewart, Charles "Wigg" Walker, Lorenzo Washington, Maurice Williams, Bob Wilson, and George Yates. These friends have informed not only the fundamental story of the music itself, but have given of themselves to secure its history.

Many museum staff members devoted time and talent to both. Space prohibits listing them all, but some deserve mention here. Vice President of Museum Services Michael Gray has been instrumental in bringing this music and work forward, beginning with his collaboration with former staff member Daniel Cooper in the museum's original *Night Train to Nashville* exhibition, presented in 2004, as well as today's effort. Director of Exhibits John Sloboda led the curatorial team. Staff contributors included Kevin Fleming, Mick Buck, Adam Iddings, Rosemary Zlokas, Shepherd Alligood, Kathleen Boyle, Julea Thomerson, Kathleen Campbell, RJ Smith, Alan Stoker, Kimberly Connors, Rachel Jacob, Dave Paulson, and Elek Horvath.

Senior Director of Editorial Paul Kingsbury, Vice President of Creative Warren Denney, Director of Creative Design Bret Pelizzari, book designer Arlie Birket, Sydney Gilbert, and Debbie Sanders deserve special recognition.

We are deeply grateful to the Metro Nashville Arts Commission and the Tennessee Arts Commission, both of which provide essential operating support that underwrites museum publications, school programs, and public programs.

WLAC disc jockey Gene Nobles is pictured on this mail-order catalog for Randy's Record Shop. COURTESY OF MIKE SMYTH. ARTIFACT PHOTO BY BOB DELEVANTE

Below are the acknowledgments from the original 2004–2005 *Night Train to Nashville* exhibition.

We are grateful to all of these contributors who helped us create this exhibit.

SPECIAL THANKS TO THE NIGHT TRAIN TO NASHVILLE ADVISORY COMMITTEE

Thomas Cain · Carol Crittenden · Charles Dungey Jr. (1938–2003) · Francis Guess · Thelma Harper · Buddy Killen · Reavis Mitchell · James Stroud · Bob Wilson

THANKS TO THE FOLLOWING FOR THEIR HELP AND SUPPORT

Theodore Acklen Jr.
Gene Allison (1934–2004)
Nelson Andrews
Morgan Babb
Barry Beckett
Babs Young Behar
Ed Benson Jr.
David Black
Connie Bradley
Mary-Ann Brandon and Fred James
William Bridgeforth
Eula Brooks
John Broven
J. Aaron Brown
Freeman Brown
Jannie Buchanan
Chucki Burke
Ednaearle Burney
Sean Carney
Freddie Carpenter
Buzz Cason
Jimmy Church
James Clemmons
David Conrad
Paul Corbin
Billy Cox
Hank Crawford
Mike Curb
Clifford Curry
Bill Dahl
Joe Davis
J. William Denny
Paul Easley
Todd Ellsworth
Colin Escott
Bebe Evans
Robert Fisher
Jim Foglesong
Richard Frank
Eddie Frierson
Earl Gaines
Pedro Garcia
Mac Gayden
Vince Gill
Al Giombetti
Andy Goodrich

Peter Guralnick
Jeff Hannusch
Emmylou Harris
Martin Hawkins
Allen Haynes
Bobby Hebb
Helen Hebb
John Heidelberg
Lon Helton
Paula Hester
Bruce Hinton
Lois Holmes
Reba Holmes
Christian Horsnell
Frank Howard
Keel Hunt
Irene Irvin
Melvin Jackson
Marion James
Ted Jarrett
Frank Jones
Johnny Jones
Henry Juszkiewicz
Ken Kanter
Clarence Kilcrease
Robert Knight
Jeff Knutson
Kevin Lavender
J.B. LeCroy
Karen Leipziger
Little Richard
Billy Lockridge
Steve Maer
Michael Manning
Jonathan Marx
Ron Miller
W. Michael Milom
James Moon
Charles Myers
Yolanda Neely
Mary Anne Nelson
Donna Nicely
James Nixon
Jim Ed Norman
Frank Oakley
Lee Olson

James Otey
Bill Purcell
Fred Reif
Margaret Richbourg
Hargus Robbins
Kenneth Roberts
David Ross
Ed Salamon
Doug Seroff
Dan Sherry
Foster Shockley
Scott Siman
Shelby Singleton Jr.
Bobby Smith
Mike Smyth
Marty Stuart
Donna Summer
Eugenia Sweeney
Larry Taylor
Shirley Trotter
Bob Tubert
Steve Turner
Tempest Utley
Aaron Varnell
Mark Wait
Margaret and Alton Warwick
Audrey and James Watkins
E.W. "Bud" Wendell
Janice Wendell
Ruth White
Kent Wildman
Brian Williams
Ernie Williams
Tim Wipperman
Deniece Wright
Ron Wynn
Cal Young
Jay Young
Jerry Zolten

BMI Archives
Carnegie Hall
Center for Creative Photography,
    University of Arizona
Center for Popular Music,
    Middle Tennessee State University

Experience Music Project
Fisk University Library Special
    Collections
Grand Ole Opry Museum
Meharry Medical College Archives,
    S. S. Kresge Learning Resources Center
Metropolitan Government Archives of
    Nashville and Davidson County
Music City Blues Society
Nashville Public Library
Showtime Music Archive
Sony/ATV Music Acuff Rose
Sun Entertainment Corporation
Sumner County Museum
Tennessee State Library and Archives
Tennessee State University,
    Special Collections and Archives
J. D. Williams Library,
    University of Mississippi
Willie Nelson's Act IV
    Videotape Library
WKRN-TV
WMDB-AM
WVOL-AM

1220 Exhibits
Anode
Bohan
DNA Creative
ESIDesign
Fastsigns, Antioch
Latocki Team Creative
Lost Highway Records
Metro Nashville Public Schools
Nashville Convention & Visitors Bureau
Nashville Scene
Sony Music Studios
SunTrust Banks, Inc.
Tower Records
WQQK-FM
WSM·AM
WSM-FM
Christine Young

FOREWORD

BY FRANK HOWARD

When I heard my first record, "Just Like Him," on the radio for the first time, I was floored. It wasn't playing on just any station, but Nashville's legendary WLAC, with a 50,000-watt signal that carried rhythm & blues music across North America, from Canada to the Caribbean.

My uncles and cousins in Indiana and Illinois tuned in to hear me sing, and of course, so did my parents, Bruce and Virginia Howard, who moved our family to Nashville from Pulaski, Tennessee, when I was seven years old. My mama told me, "Your daddy says you're singing that devil music. But I like that song."

Even for a deacon's son, the call of the city's R&B scene was impossible to resist. Things were really jumping in Nashville in the 1960s. The nightclubs on Jefferson Street and Fourth Avenue were filled with people all the time, and the stages were packed with talent. Jimi Hendrix was at Club Del Morocco, and Johnny Sneed and the guys were at Club Baron. You could find my group, Frank Howard & the Commanders, at the Stealaway or the New Era Club.

Starting in 1964, we weren't just singing onstage, but on television sets, when *Night Train* began airing on Fridays at midnight on Nashville's WLAC-TV.

Arriving six years before *Soul Train, Night Train* was an all-Black R&B show. It had a good host ("Noble B here, thanking you for being there!") and just to be in that studio, to look around and see all these artists—the Hytones, the Avons, Peggy Gaines, Jimmy Church—it was just a joy to see us on television.

If I wasn't on the road, I'd go over to my parents' house, and together we'd watch *Night Train*, or a later program called *The!!!!Beat,* which we taped performances for in Dallas. They'd point and say, "Bubba's on television!" My dad's objections to rhythm & blues kind of faded away after our first record.

In a few short years, the neon lights in our corner of Nashville would fade as well. "Urban renewal" projects and the construction of Interstate 40 tore Jefferson Street apart. In the decades that followed, the music we'd made was becoming a lost piece of history.

It was 2003 when I heard about the Country Music Hall of Fame and Museum's plans for *Night Train to Nashville*, an exhibit and compilation album dedicated to Nashville rhythm & blues from 1945 to 1970. At first, I did not think they would tell the *real* story about our music. I did not believe they could truthfully and effectively tell this story.

Man, was I wrong. The exhibit planners—I called them "musical archaeologists"—left no stone unturned and brought Nashville's R&B legacy back to life. I lent them records, photographs, film footage, and other mementoes I'd kept in my basement for decades. After seeing artifacts and photographs provided by others in the community, I was glad they also helped make it a great exhibit. The *Night Train* albums featured dozens of talents I once shared the stage and studio with—and the Grammy-winning first volume features myself and the Commanders on the cover.

In the twenty years since the release of *Night Train to Nashville*, I have heard from people around the world, and I know my peers have as well.

Some people told us they used to "sneak" viewings of the *Night Train* TV show, and tuned into the sounds of WLAC and WVOL. Many others—even lifelong Nashvillians—told us they had no idea this historic music scene ever existed. I'm glad they do now.

Frank Howard

RIGHT: **Frank Howard onstage, mid-1960s.**

9

INTRODUCTION

"Nashville really jumps!" sang Cecil Gant in 1946. Gant would know, for he was one of many stars playing rhythm & blues in the emerging capital of country music. During the years when Nashville grew into its title of Music City USA, African American artists such as Little Richard and Jimi Hendrix spent hours of bandstand apprenticeship in Nashville's Black nightclubs. At the same time, Nashville station WLAC blasted rhythm & blues across half the United States when most national radio considered the music taboo, and Black and white musicians made hit records together in the Nashville studios in tacit disregard of segregation. How their music affected American culture and Music City to this day are questions you might ask yourself as you explore the exhibition *Night Train to Nashville: Music City Rhythm & Blues Revisited* in the pages of this catalog.

"If some Southerners could have segregated the airwaves, they would have. But the beautiful part is that airwaves are free."

—B. B. KING

LEFT: **Reel-to-reel tape of Johnny Bragg recordings.**
COURTESY OF MISTI BRAGG
ARTIFACT PHOTO BY BOB DELEVANTE

OPPOSITE PAGE: **Cecil Gant, at piano, recording with a crew of Nashville musicians in the WSM studio (l to r: Charley Grant, Farris Coursey, Jack Charamella, Ted Swinney, Cecil Gant), late 1940s.**

CLUB DEL MOROCCO
TEDDY'S SPORTMANS CLUB
NASHVILLE, TENNESSEE

D. BLACK

CITY SOUNDS
ORIGINS OF NASHVILLE R&B

The term "rhythm & blues," or "R&B," came into common usage in the late 1940s to describe an African American popular music that evolved primarily from prewar jazz, blues, and gospel. In segregated Nashville, jazz and blues flourished in Black nightclubs and theaters, while the gospel influence took hold in churches. Many who played the music learned their craft in the rigorous education programs of the city's Black high schools and colleges.

Club Del Morocco's owner, Theodore "Uncle Teddy" Acklen, had miniature baseball bats made as promotional items.
COURTESY OF THEODORE ACKLEN JR. ARTIFACT PHOTO BY BOB DELEVANTE

TOP LEFT: Brown's Dinner Club and Hotel, Jefferson Street, mid-1950s.
COURTESY OF FISK UNIVERSITY FRANKLIN LIBRARY'S SPECIAL COLLECTIONS

TOP RIGHT: Boxer Joe Louis at Club Del Morocco, Jefferson Street, 1940s.
COURTESY OF THEODORE ACKLEN JR.

OPPOSITE PAGE: Colored YMCA—Fourth Avenue North and Deaderick.
COURTESY OF THE TENNESSEE STATE LIBRARY AND ARCHIVES

This view of the Bijou Theater appeared on a 1908 postcard.
COURTESY OF NASHVILLE PUBLIC LIBRARY, THE NASHVILLE ROOM

"Pit, Pat, and Poke" (Vesther Cunningham, Irene Jackson, Goldie Stone), dancers with Jerrie Jackson's Hep Cats, 1940s.
COURTESY OF IRENE (JACKSON) IRVIN

BLACK ENTERTAINMENT DISTRICTS

Reflecting years of urban migration, enforced segregation, and general demographic shifts, much of Nashville's Black entertainment centered on two streets: Fourth Avenue North and Jefferson. Both districts housed numerous theaters, nightclubs, eateries, and Black-oriented businesses.

BIJOU THEATER

In 1916, after a three-year dormancy, the Bijou Theater on Fourth Avenue North reopened as a Black-oriented venue. As part of the Theater Owners Booking Association, or TOBA, circuit during the 1920s and 1930s, the white-owned Bijou brought in renowned African American performers such as blues singer Bessie Smith. Nashville jazz great Adolphus "Doc" Cheatham played in the Bijou's orchestra pit as a teenager, and for many years local impresario Jerrie Jackson hosted a vaudeville-style program at the Bijou, through which many of the city's Black entertainers passed.

CONTINUED ON PAGE 16

"I couldn't work for the whites, you understand that, so the only way I could get any experience was sitting in the [Bijou] pit with the band and playing the shows ... because I wanted to learn more about singers, blues singers and all that."
—JAZZ MUSICIAN DOC CHEATHAM

CECIL GANT
"Nashville Jumps"

Bullet 250—released 1946 | writer: Cecil Gant

Billed as the "G.I. Sing-Sation" during World War II, Nashville-bred pianist Cecil Gant caused a national sensation with his enduring blues ballad "I Wonder," recorded in 1944 in California. Back in Nashville, Gant pounded out this blues-boogie tribute to his hometown for Bullet Records, Nashville's first significant independent record company. "Nashville Jumps" launched Bullet's "sepia" series, which would include early discs by B. B. King, Wynonie Harris, and Rufus Thomas, among others.

CONTINUED FROM PAGE 14

"Looking back on it, I think [the Bijou] did a lot for, I'll say the Black community. It gave them something of their own to see, and enjoy. And that's what they did. And they really supported it. They really did."

—BIJOU DANCER IRENE JACKSON

BIJOU CHORUS LINE
The chorus-line dancers with Jerrie Jackson's Hep Cats were regular performers at the Bijou. They included Jackson's wife Irene (far left) and his daughter Geraldine (seated on front dancer's shoulders).

(Back, l to r) Irene Jackson, Alice Pecolia Delk, Ophelia (last name not known), Georgia Burks, Georgia Mai Foster, Goldie Stone;
(front) Mary Parrish, Geraldine Jackson (on Parrish's shoulders)
COURTESY OF IRENE (JACKSON) IRVIN

BESSIE SMITH LETTER AND PHOTO
Pioneering blues singer Bessie Smith sent this handwritten letter and photo
to Nashville-based Hatch Show Print in 1927.

ARTIFACT PHOTO BY BOB DELEVANTE

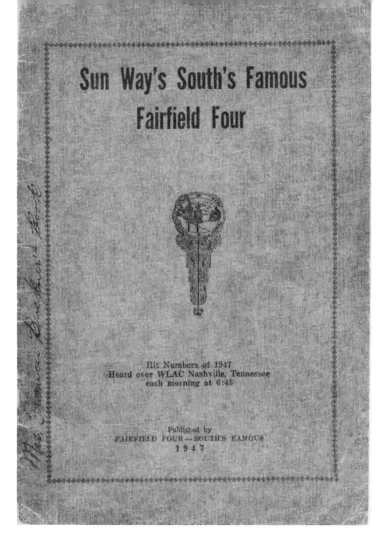

GOSPEL

Though frequently risqué lyrics and the nightclub lifestyle made R&B objectionable to many gospel music listeners, R&B singers drew much from the vocal techniques of gospel groups and in many instances emerged from their ranks. Renowned within that gospel tradition, Nashville's Fairfield Four became nationally prominent when the CBS radio network picked up their 1940s broadcasts over local station WLAC.

FAIRFIELD FOUR PAMPHLET
TOP RIGHT: This 1947 publication contains the lyrics to songs such as the Fairfield Four's signature gospel anthem "Don't Let Nobody Turn You Round."
COURTESY OF JERRY ZOLTEN

TOP LEFT: The Fairfield Four, c. 1947. Bottom row (l to r): Sam McCrary, James S. Hill, George Gracie; top row (l to r): Rufus Carrethers, Willie Frank Lewis, Rev. Edward "Preacher" Thomas.
COURTESY OF JERRY ZOLTEN

JAZZ

Known until 1968 as Tennessee A&I (Tennessee Agricultural and Industrial State Normal College), Nashville's Tennessee State University, a historically Black institution, prided itself on having one of the top jazz education programs in the country. Longtime band director Jordan "Chick" Chavis recruited heavily in Memphis and elsewhere for the school's Tennessee State Collegians jazz ensemble. In 1949, readers of the influential Black newspaper the *Pittsburgh Courier* voted the Collegians the nation's top college dance band, for which honor they performed at Carnegie Hall.

TENNESSEE STATE AT CARNEGIE HALL
TOP LEFT: This original Carnegie Hall program is from the 1949 concert during which the Tennessee State Collegians performed.

COURTESY OF CARNEGIE HALL

TENNESSEE STATE COLLEGIANS
Various members of the Tennessee State Collegians jazz band seen here (c. 1947–1948) were also active in Nashville R&B. Two months after the Collegians' 1949 performance at Carnegie Hall, a tragic tour bus accident took the lives of drummer Paul Kidd and business manager James Welch (not pictured).

FRONT ROW: (l to r) Eugene Carruthers (vocals); John Armstead, John Reed, Andy Goodrich, Samuel Ford, George Hunter (saxophones); Estil "Glen" Covington (vocals); SECOND ROW: Theophilus Griffin (standing, saxophone); Prince Shell (vibraphone); Walter Brown, Willie Weaver, Thomas Woods, Thomas Brooks (trombones); Nelson Jackson (piano); Jordan "Chick" Chavis (standing, leader); THIRD ROW: Henry Thompson, Floyd Jones, Earle "Sonny" Turner, James "Doc" Kendricks (trumpets); Clifford McCray (bass); BACK: Paul Kidd (drums).

COURTESY OF TENNESSEE STATE UNIVERSITY SPECIAL COLLECTIONS UNIT

19

ROCK THE HOUSE
NASHVILLE'S LIVE R&B SCENE

In Nashville, live rhythm & blues shook the floorboards at venues that included everything from nightclub gambling joints to the otherwise staid War Memorial Auditorium. A major stop on the southern touring circuit, sometimes derisively called the "chitlin circuit," Nashville routinely drew the top R&B acts of the day while nurturing the city's finest homegrown talent. Kept apart by the rigid dictates of segregation, young Black and white R&B fans aimed to share their joy in the music, even as the civil rights movement placed ever greater pressure on Nashville to end those laws.

CONTINUED ON PAGE 23

> "I used to work in Nashville quite a bit when I was young. I used to come in and work because that's where I really made my $100 a week at. I didn't make $100 a week nowhere but there, really."
>
> —LITTLE RICHARD

RIGHT: R&B singer Little Willie John headlined this Nashville show the year after his hit "Fever" topped the charts.
COURTESY OF DAVID EWING. ARTIFACT PHOTO BY BOB DELEVANTE

OPPOSITE PAGE: Club Del Morocco, Nashville, 1944.
COURTESY OF THEODORE ACKLEN JR. PHOTO BY GEORGE ANDERSON

TENNESSEE

E2-KW-3765
Babb Music
B.M.I.

Vocal:
Christine Kittrell

SITTIN' HERE DRINKING
(Kittrell)
CHRISTINE KITTRELL
with Band
128-45

CHRISTINE KITTRELL
"Sittin' Here Drinking"

Tennessee 128—released 1952 | writer: Christine Joygena Kittrell

Though less well known today than her contemporaries Ruth Brown, Etta James, and Lavern Baker, Nashville native Christine Kittrell recorded a number of splendid sides that should have led to a more glittering career. Kittrell scored her most successful record with this sad, low-down blues number, featuring Louie Brooks's jazzy sax riffs. At a contentious recording session with producer Ted Jarrett, Kittrell wrote the song while taking a break to have a drink in the studio office. "Ted came in and wanted to know what I was doing," Kittrell told Jarrett biographer Ruth White. "They were waiting for me. I told him, 'I'm sittin' here drinking.' And it hit me! I snatched my feet off the desk. Ted was standing there bitching, and I was writing."

CONTINUED FROM PAGE 20

JIM CROW SEATING

During the 1950s, R&B package shows often played large Nashville venues, such as the Ryman Auditorium and the Sulphur Dell baseball stadium. These star galas drew R&B's growing white fan base as well as Black audiences, but "Jim Crow" segregation dictated the two races be kept apart inside the venues. Organized protest at Nashville lunch counters in 1960 would help bring the Jim Crow era to an end.

CONTINUED ON PAGE 25

SEGREGATED SHOW TIMES
The Drifters perform at Nashville's War Memorial Auditorium in 1957.
A newspaper blurb from the time stated "the 7:30 performance will be for Negroes and the 9:30 performance for whites."

PHOTO BY ELMER WILLIAMS

RYMAN RHYTHM
This program is from a mid-1950s R&B extravaganza held at Nashville's Ryman Auditorium. Black and white audience members were required to sit on separate floors of the building.

COURTESY OF J. AARON BROWN

Vocal: Gay Crosse
Babb Music (BMI)

7008
(E2KB-6074-2)

NO BETTER FOR YOU
(Crosse)

GAY CROSSE
and the Good Humor Six

REPUBLIC RECORDS · NASHVILLE TENNESSEE

GAY CROSSE & THE GOOD HUMOR SIX
"No Better for You"

Republic 7008—released 1952 | writers: Gay Crosse and Que Martin

Gay Crosse arrived in Nashville in 1952 with a group that included saxophonist and future jazz titan John Coltrane. Coltrane played on a handful of Nashville R&B recordings, and his solo on this record showed signs of his later brilliance. A vocalist-saxophonist who stylistically resembled Louis Jordan, Crosse launched his own career on a number of West Coast and Chicago labels. Pianist Stanley "Stash" O'Laughlin, bassist Alvin Jackson, drummer Oliver Jackson, and trumpeter Tommy Turrentine (brother of jazz great Stanley Turrentine) rounded out the band.

CONTINUED FROM PAGE 23

MAGIC GUITAR

In 1962, after completing military service at Fort Campbell, Kentucky, guitarist Jimi Hendrix and his friend bassist Billy Cox moved to Nashville. Drawn by the local R&B scene, they apprenticed in Printers Alley and in a long residency at the Club Del Morocco on Jefferson Street.

> **"That's where I learned to play really . . . Nashville."**
> **—JIMI HENDRIX**

JIMI IN NASHVILLE

INSET: Billy Cox and Jimi Hendrix appeared at the Jolly Roger in Printers Alley in 1963.

BELOW: Jimi Hendrix and Billy Cox perform with the King Kasuals at the Del Morocco, two nights before Christmas, 1962. (l to r) Jimi Hendrix, unidentified drummer, Alphonso Young, Billy Cox, Buford Majors, Raymond Belt (doing splits).

COURTESY OF EXPERIENCE MUSIC PROJECT © 2000

JOLLY ROGER
FEATURING
BILLY COX and the SANDPIPERS
Also
JIMMY HENDRIX
AND HIS MAGIC GUITAR
NO COVER—NO MINIMUM SUNDAY thru THURSDAY
YOU MUST BE 21 AND PROVE IT

HOUSE ACTS

Many of the Nashville R&B clubs featured house acts who might play on a weekly basis for months or years on end when not performing out of town. Indeed, theirs is a street-level story of fame and musical impact rarely reflected in the charts and record sales to which music history is often reduced. Earl Gaines held forth at the Nashville's Sugar Hill, for instance, while at Club Stealaway the vocal trio Frank Howard & the Commanders sang Wednesday nights from nine until one in the morning.

JUST LIKE THEM
LEFT: **Frank Howard & the Commanders (l to r: Charlie Fite, Frank Howard, Herschel Carter) at Club Stealaway.** ABOVE: **the trio toasts the 1964 release of their first record, "Just Like Him." Howard's own copy is seen here.**
RECORD AND PHOTO COURTESY OF FRANK HOWARD

26

BLOWING THROUGH TOWN

Centrally located in the heart of the Mid-South, Nashville saw virtually every major R&B act of the time step across its stages. Whether it was the Club Baron on Jefferson, the old Sulphur Dell baseball park, or the New Era Club, out-of-town acts generally found a ready, raucous audience in Music City.

SUGAR HILL BLUES
Earl Gaines (far right) played the Ryman Auditorium and Carnegie Hall with the Top Ten Revue of 1955. Here he's seen at Nashville's Sugar Hill with (l to r) Stanley Hemphill, Clifford McCray, James Stuart, and Buford Majors.
COURTESY OF EARL GAINES AND FRED JAMES

Advance
Adm. $2.00
N⁰ 96996
Sun. Apr. 29.
Good Only
8:30 P.M.
Rain Check
Keep This

SUPERSONIC ATTRACTIONS
- PRESENTS
SAM COOKE
"Twisting The Night Away"

Admit 1
Sulphur Dell
Ball Park
Sun. Apr. 29
8:30 Show
Advance
Adm. $2.00
Inc. Tax

NASHVILLE TICKET
R&B great Sam Cooke was in his prime when this ticket was printed for a Nashville show in 1962.
ARTIFACT PHOTO BY BOB DELEVANTE

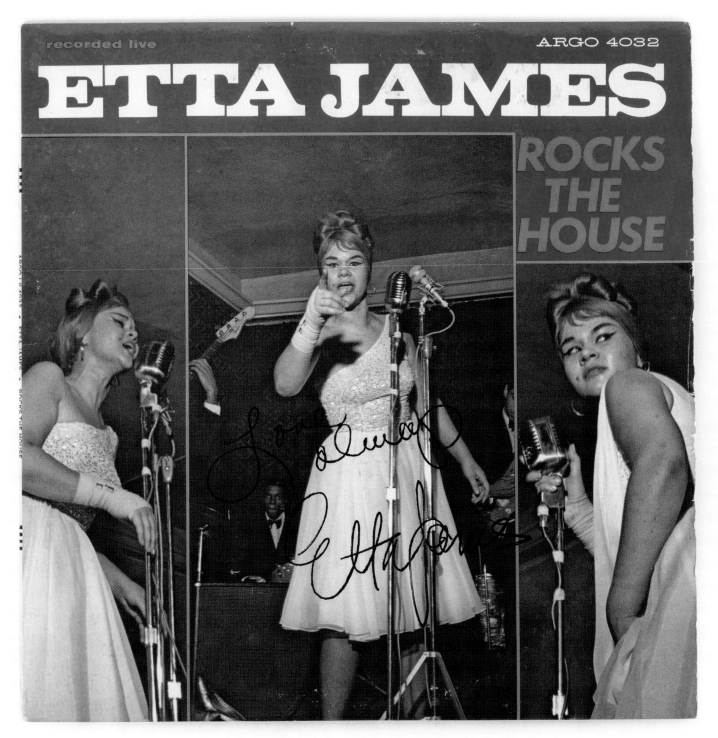

ETTA ROCKS NASHVILLE

Etta James recorded this live album at Nashville's New Era Club in 1963. According to her producer, the Nashville venue was chosen "because of the atmosphere generated by the public who patronize this club." James autographed the album for a fan when she appeared at the Ryman Auditorium years later.

ARTIFACT PHOTO BY BOB DELEVANTE

RHYTHM KINGS

One of many Memphis musicians drawn to Nashville to study at Tennessee State University, saxophonist Hank Crawford led an R&B group called Little Hank & the Rhythm Kings that often played the Subway Lounge in Printers Alley. After Ray Charles hired Crawford, the saxophonist's first return trip to Nashville with Charles's band was for the gig pictured here at local venue Maceo's.

> "Nashville holds a dear place in my heart . . . Ray Charles asked me to join his band after hearing me there. A lot happened for me during that time."
>
> **—HANK CRAWFORD**

SUBWAY LOUNGE TO STARDOM
After leaving Ray Charles's group in 1963, Hank Crawford led his own jazz outfit, which utilized matching, hand-painted bandstands including this one.
COURTESY OF HANK CRAWFORD
ARTIFACT PHOTO BY BOB DELEVANTE

BROTHER RAY IN NASHVILLE
RIGHT: Ray Charles and band at Maceo's in Nashville, c. 1959. (l to r): Edgar Willis, Ray Charles, Milt Turner (obscured), David "Fathead" Newman, Hank Crawford (looking back), Marcus Belgrave, the Raeletts (Margie Hendrix, Pat Lyles, Gwendolyn Berry, Darlene McCrae).
COURTESY OF LARRY TAYLOR

After Johnny Bragg died in 2004, his daughter, Misti, found these reel-to-reel tapes, which include demos and rehearsals of Bragg's original songs.
COURTESY OF MISTI BRAGG.
ARTIFACT PHOTO BY BOB DELEVANTE

HEY JOHN R!

RADIO, RECORDS, RHYTHM & BLUES

| "WLAC was all we ever listened to."
—JAMES BROWN

In 1946, as WLAC-Nashville had begun to strategically plan the broadcast of Black music, several local African American college students are said to have handed disc jockey Gene Nobles, who was white, a stack of R&B and jazz records imploring him to play them.

"Would you play some of our music?" With those words, and from that night forward, WLAC's 50,000-watt clear signal bounced across the stratosphere as the most powerful force in R&B broadcasting in America. This occurred just as Nashville began to assert itself as a major recording center, not only for country music but also for R&B on Excello Records and other labels heard on WLAC. With the 1951 addition of WSOK, a full-time Black programming station, mid-twentieth century Nashville rocked on wax and wavelength to a beat that would literally change the world.

CONTINUED ON PAGE 34

OPPOSITE PAGE: The WLAC jocks, 1968. Seated (l to r): John "John R" Richbourg, Gene Nobles, Bill "Hoss" Allen, Herman Grizzard. Standing: Don Whitehead, the first African American hired as a full-time announcer at WLAC.
COURTESY OF FAMILY OF HOSS ALLEN

THE PRISONAIRES
"Just Walkin' in the Rain"

Sun 186—released 1953 | writers: Johnny Bragg and Robert S. Riley

Tenor singer Johnny Bragg formed the Prisonaires vocal group while serving time at Nashville's strictly segregated Tennessee State Penitentiary on rape convictions that he claimed were false. Tennessee governor Frank Clement championed the Prisonaires as part of his prison reform efforts. Held up as examples of rehabilitation at work, Bragg's group routinely performed for dignitaries and celebrities at the governor's mansion. With one guard and a trustee driver, the Prisonaires traveled to Memphis in 1953 to record the evocative, melancholy ballad "Just Walkin' in the Rain" for Sun Records. Written by Bragg and another inmate, Robert Riley, the song became a #2 pop hit for Johnnie Ray three years later.

ARTHUR GUNTER
"Baby Let's Play House"

Excello 2047—released 1954 | writer: Arthur Gunter

Backed by members of Kid King's Combo, Nashville-born guitarist Arthur Gunter recorded this countrified blues number at the small studio located inside Ernie's Record Mart, the downtown store owned by Excello Records owner Ernie Young. The disc reached #12 on *Billboard*'s R&B chart in 1955. That same year Elvis Presley covered the song for Sun—slightly altering the lyrics—resulting in Presley's first chart record. "My first royalty check off Presley's record was six and a half thousand dollars," Gunter recalled. "I was satisfied with that."

TENNESSEE RECORDS

Founded in 1949, Tennessee Records was among Nashville's first independent record labels. The company recorded Nashville R&B stalwarts such as Christine Kittrell and Louis Brooks & His Hi-Toppers.

ERNIE'S RECORD MART

Located in downtown Nashville, Ernie's Record Mart sold mail-order R&B records to listeners of *Ernie's Record Parade*, hosted by disc jockey John "John R" Richbourg on WLAC. Ernie's record orders are said to have reached a thousand per day by the 1960s.

BELOW: The Prisonaires visit with young Bob Clement, future United States congressman, at the Tennessee governor's mansion, 1953. (Clockwise from top left) John Drue, Marcel Sanders, William Stewart, Ed Thurman, corrections official James Proctor, Bob Clement, and Johnny Bragg.

TOP: Guitarist and engineer Larry Taylor at the Excello controls, circa late 1950s.
COURTESY OF LARRY TAYLOR

BOTTOM: Louis Brooks & His Hi-Toppers: (l to r) Lovell "Knott" Phillips, Ollie Brown, Louis (Louie) Brooks, Andy Davis.
COURTESY OF EULA BROOKS

HAPPY JACK
Lead voice in the gospel group the Radio Four and program director at WSOK/
WVOL, Morgan Babb broadcasts under his R&B moniker "Happy Jack" from Ernie's
Record Mart, downtown Nashville, c. 1954.
COURTESY OF DR. MORGAN BABB

EXCELLO RECORDS

In 1951–1952, Ernie's Record Mart owner Ernie Young launched the Nashboro and Excello record labels. Nashboro would become a prolific gospel imprint with groups such as the Skylarks, while Excello would release R&B classics such as Arthur Gunter's 1954 "Baby Let's Play House," which Elvis Presley covered.

ABOVE: Nashville native Jackie Shane was a pioneering artist. In 1960, she relocated to Canada, where she became a star, returning to her hometown to perform on *Night Train* in 1965. This poster promoted an appearance by Shane in 1960.
ARTIFACT PHOTO BY BOB DELEVANTE

TOP LEFT: Promotional item for the Nashville gospel group the Skylarks: (l to r) Robert Crenshaw, James Hill, Lindsay Starks, Isaac Freeman.
COURTESY OF JERRY ZOLTEN.

BOTTOM LEFT: Excello LP by Nashville's Roscoe Shelton.

WLAC 50,000-WATT NIGHT SKYWAVE COVERAGE

.1 mV/m SECONDARY SERVICE

.5 mV/m PRIMARY SERVICE

B. SCOTT BAXTER
AND ASSOCIATES
P. O. BOX 413
BRENTWOOD, TENN. 37027

FOR SALE BY U. S. GEOLOGICAL SURVEY, WASHINGTON   D. C.

INTERIOR-GEOLOGICAL SURVEY, WASHINGTON, D. C.

Polyconic projection.

WLAC COMMERCIALS

During the golden era of WLAC's R&B programming, the jocks built a memorable catalog of pitches for products, including White Rose Petroleum Jelly, Royal Crown Hairdressing, and the infamous WLAC baby chicks.

WLAC COVERAGE MAP
ABOVE: This map detailing WLAC's nighttime coverage cuts off before Jamaica, where the station's R&B programming was so popular that an early Jamaican recording studio was named Randy's, after WLAC sponsor Randy's Record Shop.
COURTESY OF FAMILY OF HOSS ALLEN

RIGHT: Randy's Record Mart, circa 1952.
COURTESY OF THE SUMNER COUNTY ARCHIVES/ALLEN HAYNES

WSOK

In December 1951, WSOK debuted on Nashville radio as one of the nation's first full-time all-Black stations. Though white-owned, WSOK featured a staff of African American announcers and Black-oriented programs with names such as *Cook's Blues, Cool Rhythms,* and *Peace in the Valley.*

> **"We buried a lot of people, and clothed a lot of people, and housed a lot of people, and fed a lot of people, and after that then the general market began to pick up and follow."**
> **—DR. MORGAN BABB**
> **FORMER WSOK/WVOL PROGRAM DIRECTOR**

Photo of WSOK listeners awaiting the arrival of Santa Claus, December 1952.

A WSOK promotional cigarette lighter, early 1950s.

A WVOL sock hop, with Morgan Babb in back spinning records as "Happy Jack."

COURTESY OF DR. MORGAN BABB

WVOL station survey featuring disc jockey Gilly Baby (Clarence Kilcrease).

COURTESY OF CHUCKI BURKE

RIGHT: A *Tennessean* advertisement the day of WSOK's on-air grand opening, December 14, 1951.

COURTESY OF CAL YOUNG

WVOL

In 1956, WSOK founder Cal Young sold the station, and its call letters changed to WVOL. The station retained its all-Black format and its community focus, however, with on-air staff routinely helping to raise emergency funds for listeners in need.

CONTINUED ON PAGE 42

LOUIS BROOKS & HIS HI-TOPPERS WITH EARL GAINES
"It's Love Baby (24 Hours a Day)"

Excello 2056—released 1955 | writer: Ted Jarrett

Tenor saxophonist Louie Brooks (credited as "Louis" on records) led a group that backed countless Nashville singers and scored a hit of their own. The jaunty R&B shuffle "It's Love Baby" reached #2 on *Billboard's* R&B chart and launched the career of lead vocalist Earl Gaines, who quickly was invited to join a traveling revue with Big Joe Turner, Etta James, and Bo Diddley. A major talent who moved to Nashville from Alabama in his teens, Gaines went on to record a number of southern blues and soul gems for various labels. "It's Love Baby" bolstered Ted Jarrett's songwriting career, as covers by Hank Ballard and Ruth Brown also reached the R&B Top Ten in 1955.

GENE ALLISON
"You Can Make It If You Try"

Vee-Jay 256—released 1957 | writer: Ted Jarrett

This inspirational ballad is Ted Jarrett's signature composition and Gene Allison's career record. Born in Pegram, Tennessee, Allison moved to nearby Nashville at age seven. The singer made his first public appearances in the Methodist church and served a brief stint with gospel stalwarts the Skylarks before Jarrett persuaded him to record R&B songs. Jarrett produced "You Can Make It If You Try" at Owen Bradley's studio on Sixteenth Avenue using trumpeter Joe Morris's band, then licensed the recording to Chicago powerhouse Vee-Jay Records. The gospel-tinged single anticipated the dawn of soul and went Top Five R&B and Top Forty pop on *Billboard*'s charts. "Vee-Jay wanted to put me on *American Bandstand*, but Dick Clark didn't like it because it was too churchy," Allison recalled. "He didn't like the organ." The Rolling Stones covered "You Can Make It If You Try" on their 1964 debut album.

CONTINUED FROM PAGE 39

NASHVILLE ARTISTS

Many Nashville R&B acts grew up in or near the city itself. Gene Allison, for instance, previously sang in local gospel groups, while the Avons (Beverly and Fran Bard, Paula Hester) joined together while attending Nashville's Pearl High School. Some, such as Marion James, remained active in Nashville music into the twenty-first century.

NASHVILLE PRODUCERS

It took committed producers to capture Nashville's R&B talent on record. Ted Jarrett, a Nashville native, and Bob Holmes, a Tennessee State University alumnus from Memphis, both wrote songs and produced records prolifically.

ABOVE: Marion James and band, Hopewell, Tennessee, c. 1971: (l to r) John Helms, James Stuart, Marion James, (unidentified), Billy Cox.
COURTESY OF MARION JAMES

TOP: Hatch Show Print poster for Gene Allison, whose 1957 Nashville hit "You Can Make It If You Try" was later covered by the Rolling Stones.
ARTIFACT PHOTO BY BOB DELEVANTE

BOTTOM: The Hytones: (l to r) Freddie Waters, Eddie Frierson, "Skeet" Alsup.
COURTESY OF FRANK HOWARD

ELF'S SOUL

Songwriters Buzz Cason ("Everlasting Love") and Bobby Russell ("Honey") started Elf Records in Nashville and scored an R&B classic with Clifford Curry's 1967 beach favorite "She Shot a Hole in My Soul."

SOUND STAGE 7

Established in 1963, Sound Stage 7 became Nashville's leading R&B label after Excello when John Richbourg of WLAC began contributing as a producer. The label roster ranged from Joe Simon to Ivory Joe Hunter to Nashville quartet the Valentines.

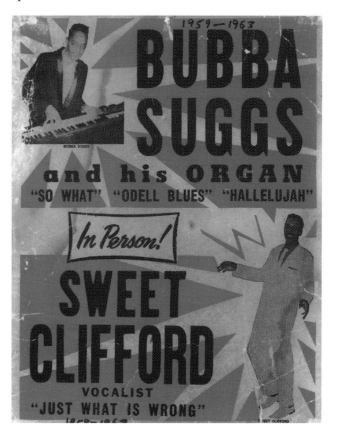

TOP: **Clifford Curry at Nashville's Centennial Park, backed by (l to r) Wade Conklin, Buzz Cason, and guitarist Mac Gayden, co-writer of "She Shot a Hole in My Soul."**

COURTESY OF CLIFFORD CURRY

BOTTOM: **Sound Stage 7 promotional photograph of the Valentines: (clockwise from top) James Moon, Paul Easley, Charles Myers, James Clemmons.**

COURTESY OF JAMES MOON

Poster for Clifford Curry in his early years as "Sweet Clifford."

COURTESY OF CLIFFORD CURRY

ALL ABOARD THE NIGHT TRAIN!

NASHVILLE'S R&B TELEVISION

Following through on the success of its Black radio programs, Music City produced two extraordinary syndicated R&B TV shows, *Night Train* and *The!!!!Beat*. Both featured some of Nashville's best R&B musicians backing some of the city's finest singers and out-of-town stars, including Otis Redding and Percy Sledge. Local Black artists such as Bobby Hebb and Audrey Bryant had pioneered on Nashville television in the 1950s, but it wasn't until *Night Train* hit the midnight Friday slot (actually 12:15 a.m. Saturday) in 1964 that a music series with an all-Black cast brought the dance beat to living-room screens.

RIGHT: This Gibson ES-345 electric guitar was used in later years by premier blues guitarist Johnny Jones, who performed in the house band on *Night Train* and *The!!!!Beat* and influenced Jimi Hendrix.
COURTESY OF JIMMY CHURCH. ARTIFACT PHOTO BY BOB DELEVANTE

OPPOSITE PAGE: This syndication ad for *Night Train* appeared in the April 6, 1966 issue of *Variety* magazine.
COURTESY OF DAVID EWING

Noble Blackwell
COURTESY OF FRANK HOWARD

NIGHT TRAIN

Produced at WLAC-TV in Nashville, *Night Train* debuted in October 1964, six years before Chicago's better-known *Soul Train.* Hosted by show creator and WVOL executive Noble Blackwell, *Night Train* boasted a house band led by musical director Bob Holmes and showcasing the fiery blues licks of guitarist Johnny Jones. Nashville talents such as Jimmy Church, the Spidells, the Hytones, and the Avons were regulars, and Jimi Hendrix appeared on *Night Train* while he was still just a backing guitarist.

CONTINUED ON PAGE 48

"It was a period of the sixties, you had demonstrations going on in Nashville, but *Night Train* offered a good ... entertainment vehicle. We had very good artists, and of course it highlighted the local artists who were very talented, and a lot of hard work went into it because we would practice at various community centers in Nashville. The Nashville Housing Authority allowed us to use the community centers where we would practice."

—*NIGHT TRAIN* HOST AND CREATOR NOBLE BLACKWELL

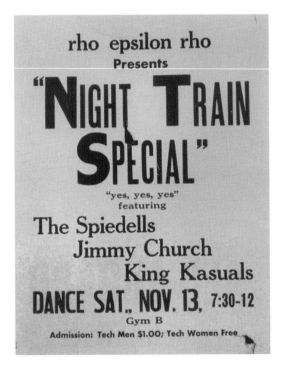

NIGHT TRAIN SPECIAL
This mid-1960s poster advertised a Tennessee Tech University concert by *Night Train* artists the Spidells (misspelled), Jimmy Church, and the King Kasuals. The Spidells (Michael Young, Lee Roy Cunningham, James Earl Smith, Nathaniel Shelton, and lead vocalist Billy Lockridge) formed their group while students at Tennessee State University. At various times, the King Kasuals included guitarists Jimi Hendrix and Johnny Jones, and bassist Billy Cox.
COURTESY OF BILLY LOCKRIDGE

THE GLADIOLAS
"Little Darlin'"

Excello 2101—released 1956 | writer: Maurice Williams

Formed in Lancaster, South Carolina, teen vocal group the Gladiolas traveled to Nashville to record this Excello classic for Ernie Young at the studio in Ernie's Record Mart. "I heard John Richbourg's show, *Ernie's Record Parade*, on WLAC," recalled Maurice Williams, who provided the memorable falsetto part. "He played the kind of music that I knew my group could sing. I got Ernie's number by calling WLAC, and Ernie said, 'If you're ever over this way, let me know you're coming and I'll set up an audition for you.' We went around to different merchants in Lancaster and raised thirty-seven dollars for our trip to Nashville, which we made in an old Chrysler, with no spare tires, in the days before interstates. I first had 'Little Darlin'' going like a straight ballad in the vein of 'This Magic Moment.' Ernie told us to make it into a calypso, telling us how to do it, because I was only sixteen and didn't know what calypso was." The Gladiolas' record reached #11 R&B and #41 pop on the *Billboard* charts, and was immediately covered by Canadian group the Diamonds, whose version sold an estimated four million copies. Soon fronting a new doo-wop group called the Zodiacs, Williams topped the pop charts in 1960 with "Stay."

CONTINUED FROM PAGE 46

THE!!!!BEAT

A little over a year after *Night Train*, the color TV extravaganza *The!!!!Beat* made its similarly formatted debut on nationally syndicated television. Hosted by WLAC-radio's Hoss Allen, the show had been conceived by the same business enterprise that backed country music's *Porter Wagoner Show*. Like *Night Train*, *The!!!!Beat* featured Nashville-based musicians, with the addition of guitarist-bandleader Clarence "Gatemouth" Brown. It was actually taped at WFAA-Dallas to take advantage of the Texas station's then-rare color capabilities.

The!!!!Beat guests (l to r) Little Milton, Joe Simon, Freddie King, Veniece Starks, and host Hoss Allen; with the Beat Boys: pianist Skippy Brooks; bassist Billy Cox; guitarist Johnny Jones; saxophonist Aaron Varnell; drummer Freeman Brown; trumpeters Arlen Mitchell, (unidentified), Harrison Calloway; bongo player Jimmy Church (obscured); and go-go dancers (unidentified), 1966.
COURTESY OF ACT IV

JIMI AND BILLY
LEFT: While learning their trade in Nashville, guitarist Jimi Hendrix and bassist Billy Cox practiced at home through this Gibson amplifier. Cox rigged the amp so they could play together, and during these practice sessions they originated songs they later recorded, such as "Freedom" and "Dolly Dagger."
ABOVE: This vest belonged to Hendrix during his star years.
COURTESY OF BILLY COX

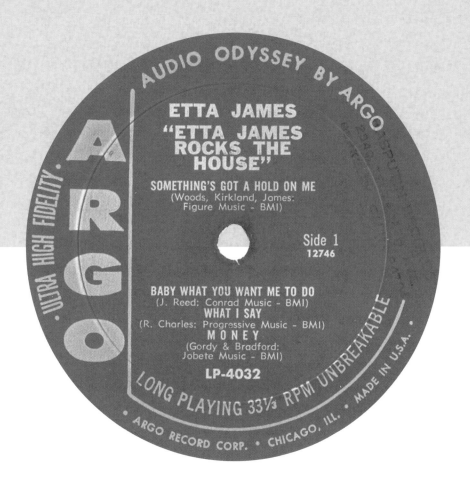

ETTA JAMES
"What'd I Say" (live)

Track from Argo LP 4032—released 1963 | writer: Ray Charles

Established by William Bridgeforth, the New Era Club perhaps was Nashville's best-known nightclub for hosting R&B chartbusters. Etta James recorded her no-holds-barred live album *Etta James Rocks the House* at the New Era on September 27 and 28, 1963, supported by her touring band. Armed with a one-track Webcor tape recorder, producer Ralph Bass captured the blues belter in her prime for Chess Records'

Argo subsidiary. In the liner notes for *Etta James Rocks the House*, Bass wrote: "The New Era Club was selected in Nashville because of the atmosphere generated by the public who patronize this club. Etta is a favorite there." A standout track on the album is James's roaring take on "What'd I Say," a 1959 #1 R&B hit for Ray Charles.

ARTHUR ALEXANDER
"Anna (Go to Him)"

Dot 16387—released 1962 | writer: Arthur Alexander Jr.

A native of Florence, Alabama, Arthur Alexander moved to Music City after his 1961 Muscle Shoals classic "You Better Move On" found a label home at Dot Records. Dot was founded in the late 1940s by Randy Wood in Gallatin, Tennessee, just north of Nashville, after his Randy's Record Shop became known to R&B fans far and wide through its sponsorship on WLAC. Produced by Dot A&R man Noel Ball and backed by Music Row session pros such as Charlie McCoy, Hargus "Pig" Robbins, Kenneth Buttrey, and the Anita Kerr Singers, Alexander cut a string of enduring country-soul gems for the label. Alexander took his self-penned "Anna (Go to Him)" to the R&B Top Ten, and the Beatles' faithful rendition on their 1963 debut album offered an early showcase for John Lennon's vocals.

ESTHER PHILLIPS
"Release Me"

Lenox #5555—released 1962 | writers: William McCall, Eddie Miller, James Pebworth, and Robert Yount

Known as "Little Esther" in the 1950s, when she was a teenage R&B hitmaker, Galveston, Texas, native Esther Phillips rekindled her faltering career with this bluesy rendition of "Release Me." Written by Oklahoma country artist Eddie Miller, "Release Me" had been a Top Ten country hit for Jimmy Heap, Kitty Wells, and Ray Price, each in 1954. In 1962, Phillips shared a Houston nightclub bill with then-little-known singer Kenny Rogers, who introduced her to his brother, fledging producer Lelan Rogers. With partner Bob Gans, Lelan started Lenox Records with Phillips as the label's charter act. Her Nashville recording of "Release Me" featured Cliff Parman–arranged strings and the Anita Kerr Singers.

RECONSIDER ME

THE COUNTRY CONNECTION

Beginning in the 1920s, many record companies divided their blues and country recordings into separate "race" and "hillbilly" series. In reality these musics shared many themes and instruments, and blues and country musicians historically learned much from one another's styles and songs. Such musical exchange between Blacks and whites carried through to the stages and studios of postwar Nashville. As explained by Nashville native Bobby Hebb, who graced the stages of both the Bijou Theater and the Grand Ole Opry, "It was very important that one understood more than one culture of music."

CONTINUED ON PAGE 56

RIGHT: **Bobby Hebb used these spoons as percussion instruments.**
ARTIFACT PHOTO BY BOB DELEVANTE

SWEENEY AND THE A-TEAM
OPPOSITE PAGE: **Jimmy Sweeney stands center among several of Music City's recording session elite: guitarist Hank Garland, bassist Floyd "Lightnin'" Chance, songwriter Boudleaux Bryant, and pianist Floyd Cramer, c. 1958.**
PHOTO BY ELMER WILLIAMS

BOBBY HEBB
"Sunny"

Philips 40365—released 1966 | writer: Bobby Hebb

Bobby Hebb is a member of a large and well-known Nashville family of musicians. His parents, William and Ovalla, were both blind and musically inclined. With his older brother Harold, Bobby performed as a child song-and-dance entertainer with the Jerrie Jackson revue at the Bijou Theater. Grand Ole Opry star Roy Acuff spotted Hebb on Owen Bradley's WSM-TV variety show and hired the teenager, who played spoons and various other instruments for Acuff's band through the early 1950s. Harold, a one-time member of the Marigolds, was knifed to death outside Club Baron on Jefferson Street on November 24, 1963, two days after John F. Kennedy was assassinated. In 1966, Hebb recorded "Sunny" with producer Jerry Ross and orchestra arranger Joe Renzetti at Bell South Studio in New York City, where Hebb was living. "All of my intentions were just to think of happier times—basically looking for a brighter day—because times were at low tide," Hebb said about writing the song. "After I wrote it, I thought 'Sunny' just might be a different approach to what Johnny [Bragg] was talking about in 'Just Walkin' in the Rain.'" The crossover smash landed Hebb a slot on the Beatles' final tour in 1966 and has become one of the most enduring popular standards of all time, with hundreds of cover versions released.

CLIFFORD CURRY
"She Shot a Hole in My Soul"

Elf Records 90002—released 1967 | writers: Mac Gayden and Chuck Neese

After recording for Excello as "Sweet Clifford," Knoxville-bred Clifford Curry met Buzz Cason and Mac Gayden, a pair of songwriter-producer-musicians who would play a pivotal role in Curry's career and in Nashville music. Cason had led the Casuals, one of the city's first white rock & roll bands, while renowned guitarist Gayden had, in his teens, backed Arthur Gunter and had also worked at Ernie's Record Mart. Gayden wrote and played guitar on this track after getting the title idea from his friend Chuck Neese. Gayden recalled,

"Chuck was driving down the road listening to WVOL, a strictly gospel and R&B station we all listened to, and he heard the disc jockey say something like 'Ooh! She put a hole in my soul!'" Cason produced the single and released it on Elf Records, an independent he started with Bobby Russell. Curry's record barely cracked the Top Fifty R&B chart but has since become something of a classic, especially on the beach-music scene in the Carolinas.

CECIL GANT, GREATEST RACE STAR RECORDS FOR BULLET

• • •

CECIL GANT

CECIL GANT, well-known Sepia star, has appeared in nearly every large night club on the West Coast. He has composed over a hundred songs, the most popular being "I Wonder," which was made popular by Woody Herman.

Cecil was born in Chattanooga, Tennessee, and has always been musical. He plays by ear and sings in a half-talking style, husky with plenty of heartbreak in it.

While in the Army, he started playing the piano and was placed in a Special Services unit on a Hospital ship which ran between the West Coast and Hawaii. Bette Davis, the well-known screen star, presented him with a citation for this service at the Hollywood U. S. O.

Among his recent compositions is the popular number, "Anna May".

Get These Releases By Cecil Gant

250—Nashville Jumps / Loose As A Goose
257—I'm All Alone / Forgive and Forget
258—Ninth Street Jive / It's The Girl
264—Every Minute of Every Hour / Boozie Boogie
265—Go To Sleep Little Baby / My, My, My
255—Train Time Blues / Sloppy Joe's

• • •

News Of BULLET Money Making RECORDS

W. E. HARVEY CO., INC.
12649 LINWOOD AVE.
DETROIT 6, MICH.
TO. 9-5950

ORDER BLANK

(Distributor's Address)

Serial No.	Name of Record	Amount

"GREATEST RACE STAR"
In 1946, Cecil Gant recorded "Nashville Jumps" for the city's Bullet Records. His success earned him the cover feature in this 1947 Bullet newsletter, which also detailed the company's country and pop triumphs.

CONTINUED ON PAGE 58

RACE AND HILLBILLY
This Decca Race Records catalog dates from 1938 and its "Hill Billy" counterpart is from 1940. Well into the 1950s, the term "race music" was routinely used as an industry catchall for recordings by Black artists.

ROBERT KNIGHT
"Everlasting Love"

Rising Sons 705—released 1967 | writers: Buzz Cason and Mac Gayden

Buzz Cason and Mac Gayden not only wrote this soul-pop perennial, but also arranged and produced Robert Knight's original recording for release on their own label, Rising Sons, which was distributed by Monument Records. Knight was born Robert Peebles in Franklin, Tennessee, just south of Nashville, and was raised by his grandparents. As a teenager, Knight formed the Paramounts, who recorded for Dot in the early 1960s. (Knight changed his name on advice from producer Noel Ball.) Knight soon formed another group, the Fairlanes, and Gayden caught the act one night when he and Knight separately were entertaining frat houses at Vanderbilt University. With a voice like Smokey Robinson's, Knight took "Everlasting Love" to the Top Twenty of both the pop and R&B charts. The song has proved to be an enduring favorite and has been covered by Carl Carlton, U2, Gloria Estefan, and various others.

CONTINUED FROM PAGE 56

SUNNY

Words and Music by BOBBY HEBB

Recorded by BOBBY HEBB
on PHILIPS RECORDS

KEYS
04715

PORTABLE MUSIC CO., INC.   75¢

ABOVE: Nashville native Bobby Hebb's signature song "Sunny" was a smash hit for him in 1966. It's been covered more than five hundred times by other artists.
COURTESY OF MIKE SMYTH

HEBB'S KITCHEN CABINET ORCHESTRA

TOP LEFT: Seen in this 1942 Nashville photo, "Hebb's Kitchen Cabinet Orchestra," as the Hebb family called themselves, included (l to r) Ednaearle, Helen, William Melvoid, Ovalla (holding Shirley Ann), William Marion, Harold, and Bobby Hebb in front. Bobby joined Roy Acuff's Grand Ole Opry troupe at age twelve and later wrote and recorded the million seller "Sunny," which earned him a spot on the Beatles' 1966 tour.
COURTESY OF HELEN HEBB

BOBBY HEBB AT THE OPRY

BOTTOM LEFT: A Grand Ole Opry radio engineer kneels to capture the sound of young Bobby Hebb tap-dancing with the Smoky Mountain Boys (l to r: Robert Lunn, Jimmie Riddle, Howdy Forrester, probably Jess Easterday, Lonnie Wilson), early 1950s. Roy Acuff leans in from the right.
GORDON GILLINGHAM PHOTOGRAPH, COURTESY OF GRAND OLE OPRY ARCHIVES

CONTINUED ON PAGE 60

JOE SIMON
"The Chokin' Kind"

Sound Stage 7 2628—released 1969 | writer: Harlan Howard

Nowhere is Nashville's country-soul liaison more apparent than here. Written by Harlan Howard, the "dean of country songwriters," "The Chokin' Kind" was a #8 country hit for Waylon Jennings in 1967. Two years later, soul stalwart Joe Simon's brassy treatment of the song went #1 R&B and #13 pop on *Billboard*'s charts. Simon's single sold a million copies and earned the singer a Grammy for Best Rhythm & Blues Vocal Performance, Male. "John Richbourg introduced me to the Nashville lyrics," Simon said. "I've written some good songs and some hit songs, but . . . I can feel the country songs so much better." Cut at Scotty Moore's Music City Recorders studio, "The Chokin' Kind" features Simon's rich, expressive vocals, Bergen White's horn arrangement, Wayne Moss's chugging bass line, and Charlie McCoy's chicken-scratch guitar riff.

CONTINUED FROM PAGE 58

LET'S TRADE A LITTLE
In 1956, high school student Audrey Bryant made Nashville TV history when she joined the cast of an otherwise all-white, teen music program hosted by local disc jockey Noel Ball. Three years later, Bryant recorded "Let's Trade a Little" with renowned session pianist Hargus "Pig" Robbins (with her in the photo) and other Music City veterans.

COURTESY OF AUDREY BRYANT WATKINS

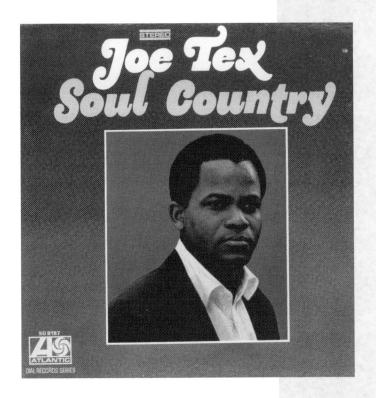

SOUL COUNTRY
In the 1960s, country producer Shelby Singleton brought R&B stars Clyde McPhatter and Ruth Brown to Nashville to record on Music Row, while Nashville publisher Buddy Killen signed Joe Tex to songwriting and record deals. "The feel in the studio was, in Nashville, really, really warm," Brown said.

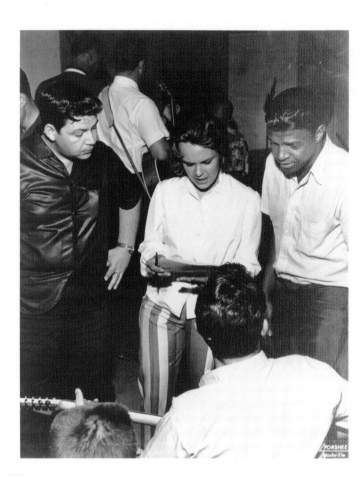

CLYDE McPHATTER SESSION
Clyde McPhatter (right) concentrates in a Nashville recording studio with producer Shelby Singleton and backup singer Margie Singleton, circa 1962. Guitarist Jerry Kennedy sits in the foreground.
COURTESY OF SUN ENTERTAINMENT CORPORATION

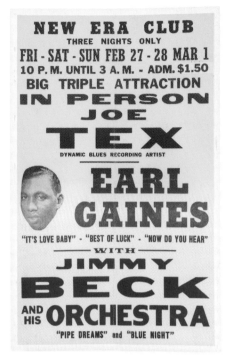

LEFT: Joe Tex frequently recorded and performed in Nashville. This Hatch Show Print poster promoted his appearances at the New Era Club in 1959.
COURTESY OF DAVID EWING
ARTIFACT PHOTO BY
BOB DELEVANTE

TEX IN NASHVILLE
Headphones on, Joe Tex listens in a Nashville studio with producer and song publisher Buddy Killen, mid-1960s.

CONTINUED ON PAGE 63

PEGGY SCOTT & JO JO BENSON
"Soul Shake"

SSS International 761—released 1969 | writers: Mira A. Smith and Margaret Lewis

Singers Peggy Scott, from Florida, and Jo Jo Benson, from Ohio, were recording separate sessions at producer Huey P. Meaux's Grits 'n' Gravy studio in Jackson, Mississippi, when they decided to work as a duo. They signed to SSS International, a soul label started by veteran producer Shelby Singleton in Nashville in 1968, a year before he purchased Sun Records from Sam Phillips. Scott and Benson recorded the dance-floor outing "Soul Shake" at Columbia Studios on Music Row. Session leader Jerry Kennedy played electric sitar, while top-shelf Nashville musicians Pete Drake, Wayne Moss, Chip Young, Charlie McCoy, David Briggs, and Kenneth Buttrey also contributed. "Soul Shake" went #13 R&B and #37 pop on the *Billboard* charts. A dozen years before MTV, Singleton spent about $2,000 making a pioneering music video for "Soul Shake," shot on 16 mm film at Nashville's Centennial Park, to promote the duo overseas.

CONTINUED FROM PAGE 61

ABOVE: Ted Jarrett's personal notebook adapted from *Cash Box* magazine cover.

RIGHT: Original sheet music for "Reconsider Me" and "The Chokin' Kind," Nashville country-soul classics recorded by Johnny Adams and Joe Simon, respectively.

MANKIND

Jerry Williams Music/
Excellorec Music
BMI
Time 2:45
Produced by
Jerry Williams, Jr.
Arranged by
Jerry Williams, Jr./
Richard Rome
Engineer:
David Johnson

Recorded at
Quinby Studios
Sheffield, Ala.

Side 1
12004
(12004-A)
Compatible
Stereo

SHE'S ALL I GOT
(J. Williams, Jr.-G. Bonds)

FREDDIE NORTH

DIST. BY NASHBORO RECORDS, NASHVILLE, TENNESSEE

FREDDIE NORTH
"She's All I Got"

Mankind 12004—released 1971 | writers: Jerry Williams and Gary Bonds

Freddie North—born Freddie Carpenter in Nashville—spent the 1960s recording for various labels, appearing on *Night Train*, and working in sales and promotion for Nashboro and Excello Records. He also recorded song demos at Tree Publishing and befriended a young recording engineer named Billy Sherrill. In 1971, North recorded "She's All I Got" in Sheffield, Alabama, for the Mankind imprint, a subsidiary of Nashboro that showcased Jerry "Swamp Dogg" Williams's productions. Co-written by Williams and Gary U.S. Bonds, North's recording hit the R&B Top Ten and crossed over to the pop Top Forty. The song found additional success on country radio when Sherrill brought the song to Epic Records artist Johnny Paycheck. "Before my record was ever released, Billy Sherrill heard the tape and fell in love with that song," North explained. "Billy told me, 'I'm cutting this thing on Paycheck. I just flat-out love it. But I don't want to get the jump on you. I want to make sure yours is out.' I told him when mine was scheduled for release. He said, 'Fine, man, I'll be looking for it, then I'm coming.' Billy and I had a good relationship."

JACKIE SHANE
"Any Other Way"

Cookin' 500—released 1962 | writer: William Bell

Jackie Shane was a Black transgender soul singer born and raised in Nashville who recorded exquisite soul music in the 1960s. "I was born a woman in this body. That's how it's always been," she once told a writer. Born in 1940, by 1962 she was performing frenzied shows in Boston when a local entrepreneur created a new label, Cookin', just to record a new song that she added to her show. Written by William Bell, "Any Other Way" is a stately ballad with Shane's voice all the way up front, opalescent supper-club soul with eerie horn chords framing a message that boils down to "I'll never be any other way—take me as I am." The song was a hit in New England and Ontario, got picked up by the Sue label, and became perhaps the biggest success Shane had in her years of singing from town to town in the U.S. and Canada. The one bit of video in existence captures her in fine form in 1965 on Nashville's groundbreaking soul show *Night Train*. Shane died in Nashville, in 2019.

EVERLASTING LOVE
R&B'S LEGACY AND LAMENT

By the late 1960s, R&B had changed America in profound ways. Black artists routinely topped the pop charts, while white musicians raised on R&B dominated the record industry. To many, these changes reflected the triumph of the integrationist ideals of Dr. Martin Luther King Jr. But others viewed the absorption of Black-originated styles into white music as one more form of racial injustice. Debate continues to this day.

In Nashville, urban change took its toll on the Black entertainment districts too, leaving behind interstate highways and musicians with ever fewer jobs. Yet the music moved forward. James Brown forged a sound of the future with "Sex Machine" and other hits recorded in Nashville studios, while Peggy Scott & Jo Jo Benson's "Soul Shake" spawned an early experiment in music video. In 1967, Robert Knight recorded the original "Everlasting Love," a song whose lasting impact attests to the enduring power of Nashville rhythm & blues.

Robert Knight album, 1967.

"'Everlasting Love' led to so many big things. I remember playing the Apollo Theater. I traveled with Joe Tex for six months. I opened for Aretha Franklin in Europe."

—ROBERT KNIGHT

OPPOSITE PAGE: This concert promotion item features both Robert Knight ("Everlasting Love") and Clifford Curry ("She Shot a Hole in My Soul").
COURTESY OF CLIFFORD CURRY

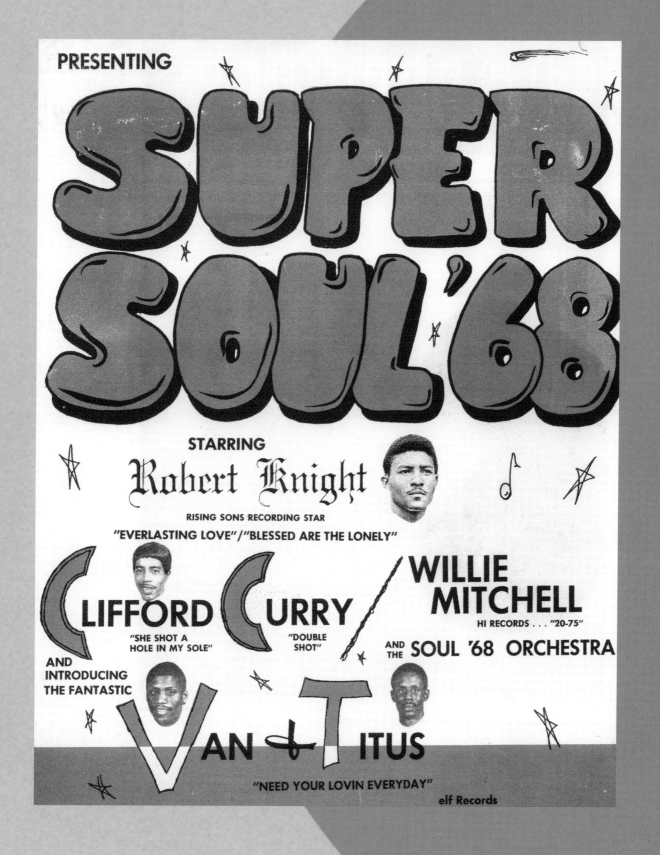

CAPITOL HILL REDEVELOPMENT

A federally funded urban renewal project, the Capitol Hill redevelopment of the 1950s did away with most of the Black commercial district centered on Fourth Avenue North. The arrival of Interstate 40 a decade later had a similar impact on Jefferson Street. In 1957, the Bijou Theater gave way to the wrecking ball and the subsequent construction on its site of the Municipal Auditorium.

THE SOUL OF MUSIC CITY

Nashville was enormously successful in developing an international reputation as Music City. But that title became so identified with country music that the city's other musical accomplishments have often been obscured. Nashville's influential rhythm & blues community played a significant role in the city becoming a world-renowned music center. That vibrant musical community was built by numerous Black Nashvillians who contributed to the city's rich history of R&B. They deserve more credit within the story of American popular music. Hear their songs. ✳

Urban renewal closes in on the Bijou Theater.
COURTESY OF METRO ARCHIVES—NASHVILLE/DAVIDSON COUNTY

JAMES BROWN
"Get Up (I Feel Like Being Like a) Sex Machine"

Starday-King 6318—released 1970 | writers: James Brown, Bobby Byrd, Ron Lenhoff

It was the night of April 25, 1970, and James Brown came straight off a triumphant Nashville Municipal Auditorium show and parked the tour bus at the Starday-King Sound Studios eight miles north on Dickerson Pike. He was hungry to record a number he had just scrawled out backstage. Brown phoned his loyal soundman Ron Lenhoff in Cincinnati and commanded him to drive to Nashville immediately. When he got there, Lenhoff cut a monster: Brown and his hot new band turning a tight live jam into an epic monochord stomp Brown called "Get Up (I Feel Like Being Like a) Sex Machine." Brown had only the month before fired his former band and restocked with a bunch of kids, including bassist William "Bootsy" Collins and his guitar-playing brother, Catfish (Phelps Collins). Called the New Breed, the band featured energy matching Brown's, and by shouting and grooving for nearly eleven glorious minutes they produced one of the foundations of funk. Brown added Lenhoff's name to the composing credits, making it worth driving to Nashville for everyone concerned.

CIRCLE GUARD

The Country Music Hall of Fame and Museum Circle Guard unites and celebrates individuals who have given their time, talent, and treasure to safeguard the integrity of country music and make it accessible to a global audience through the Museum. The Circle Guard designation ranks as the grandest distinction afforded to those whose unwavering commitment to the Museum protects the legacies of the members of the Country Music Hall of Fame, and, by extension, the time-honored achievements of all who are part of the country music story.

2024 GUARD

Steve Turner, Founder

Kyle Young, Commander General

David Conrad

Bill Denny

Ken Levitan

Mary Ann McCready

Mike Milom

Ken Roberts

Seab Tuck

Jerry B. Williams

"Take especially good care of yourself, and be good to your neighbor!"

—**NOBLE BLACKWELL**

Geraldine Jackson, 700 block of Gay Street, Nashville.
COURTESY OF IRENE (JACKSON) IRVIN